Learning to read. Reading to learn!

LEVEL ONE Sounding It Out Preschool–Kindergarten
For kids who know their alphabet and are starting to sound out words.

learning sight words • beginning reading • sounding out words

LEVEL TWO Reading with Help Preschool–Grade 1
For kids who know sight words and are learning to sound out new words.

expanding vocabulary • building confidence • sounding out bigger words

LEVEL THREE Independent Reading Grades 1–3
For kids who are beginning to read on their own.

introducing paragraphs • challenging vocabulary • reading for comprehension

LEVEL FOUR Chapters Grades 2–4
For confident readers who enjoy a mixture of images and story.

reading for learning • more complex content • feeding curiosity

Ripley Readers Designed to help kids build their reading skills and confidence at any level, this program offers a variety of fun, entertaining, and unbelievable topics to interest even the most reluctant readers. With stories and information that will spark their curiosity, each book will motivate them to start and keep reading.

Vice President, Licensing & Publishing Amanda Joiner
Editorial Manager Carrie Bolin

Editor Jordie R. Orlando
Designer Luis Fuentes
Text Carrie Bolin
Reprographics Bob Prohaska

President Andy Edwards
Chief Commercial Officer Brett Clarke
**Vice President, Global Licensing &
  Consumer Products** Cassie Dombrowski
Vice President, Creative Dov Ribnick
Senior Athlete Manager Ricky Melnik
**Global Accounts & Activation Manager,
  Consumer Products** Andrew Hogan
Art Director & Graphic Designer Josh Geduld
Special Thanks Travis Pastrana

Published by Ripley Publishing 2019

10 9 8 7 6 5 4 3 2 1

Copyright © 2019 Nitro Circus

ISBN: 978-1-60991-280-2

For more information regarding permission, contact:
VP Licensing & Publishing
Ripley Entertainment Inc.
7576 Kingspointe Parkway, Suite 188
Orlando, Florida 32819
Email: publishing@ripleys.com
www.ripleys.com/books

Manufactured in China in May 2019.

First Printing

Library of Congress Control Number: 2019903092

PUBLISHER'S NOTE
While every effort has been made to verify the accuracy of the
entries in this book, the Publisher cannot be held responsible
for any errors contained in the work. They would be glad to
receive any information from readers.

WARNING
Some of the stunts and activities are undertaken by experts
and should not be attempted by anyone without adequate
training and supervision.

PHOTO CREDITS

Cover (bkg) © Evgeny Karandaev/Shutterstock.com, (l) © Mark Watson/nitrocircus.com;
3 (l) © Mark Watson/nitrocircus.com; **4-5** (dp) © Nate Christenson/Nitro Circus; **5** © Andre
Nordheim/Nitro Circus; **7** © Chris Tedesco/Nitro Circus; **11** © Chris Tedesco/Nitro Circus;
16-17 (dp) © Josh Chapel/Southcreek Global/ZUMA Press, Inc./Alamy Stock Photo; **19** Lisa
Blumenfeld/Getty Images; **21** Courtesy of Nitro Circus; **22** © Chris Tedesco/Nitro Circus; **23** © Chris
Tedesco/Nitro Circus; **24-25** (dp) © Mark Watson/www.inciteimages.com; **26** Harry How/
Getty Images; **27** Jason Smith/Getty Images; **30-31** (dp) © Mark Watson for Nitro Circus Live/
www.nitrocircuslive.com

Key: t = top, b = bottom, c = center, l = left, r = right, sp = single page, dp = double page,
bkg = background

All other photos are courtesy of Nitro Circus and Travis Pastrana. Every attempt has been made
to acknowledge correctly and contact copyright holders, and we apologize in advance for any
unintentional errors or omissions, which will be corrected in future editions.

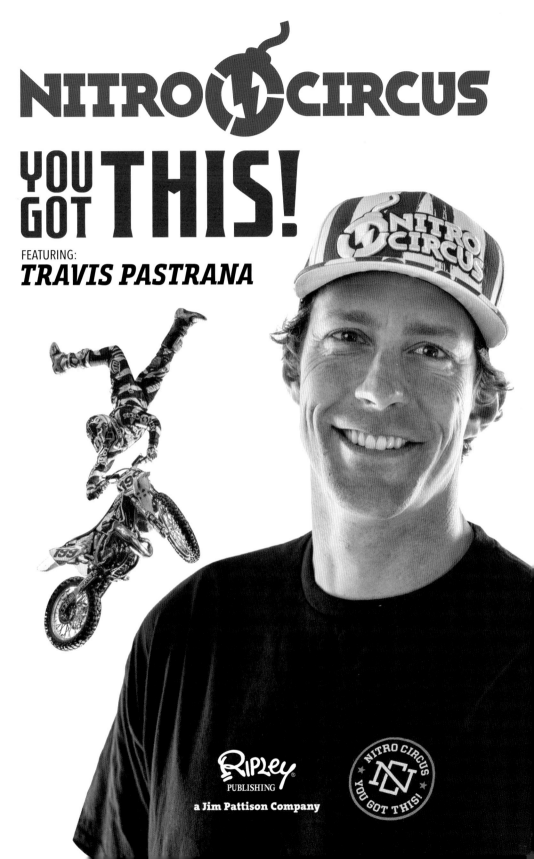

Travis Pastrana loves his job! He is the ringleader of Nitro Circus.

He leads all the action sports
athletes in new adventures
every day.

YOU GOT THIS

His motto is "You Got This!"
Travis likes to inspire people
to always believe in themselves.

Travis has lived by his motto his entire life.

He started riding a motorbike when he was only four!

You got this, little Travis!

Sometimes it was hard for Travis to believe in himself.

When he was eight, he couldn't do a backflip on a trampoline. Everyone else in his family could.

"I thought I would never learn how to flip," says Travis. "Now I can do double backflips on dirt bikes!"

Travis loved riding so much!
He started to ride in contests.
He was nine the first time he
won the Loretta Lynn National
Amateur crown.

Travis won this award five times!

Winning awards was great. Travis kept working hard. He remembered his motto and believed in himself.

Then he did something no one else had ever done. He became the World Freestyle Champion at the age of 14!

He has also won 17 X Games medals in his career. Eleven of those medals were gold!

Travis won a lot of awards. But he wanted to do more.

"If I don't have something challenging to do," he says, "I get bored."

At the 2006 X Games, he performed a world first stunt. He was the first to land a double backflip on a motorbike!

Travis loved doing something no one else had ever done. He wanted to do it every day.

"I've always followed my heart. It's always led me in the direction that made me happy," says Travis.

So, Travis followed his heart and created Nitro Circus.

There are lots of things Travis loves about Nitro Circus. The thing he loves best is that he and his friends can be together.

They get to do what they love almost every day. They ride bikes, motorcycles, skateboards, and crazy machines everywhere they go!

The friends travel all over the world. They always try to do new world first tricks.

Everyone tries hard to jump as high and ride as fast as they can!

Travis loves action sports! But he knows that they can also be dangerous. He has gotten hurt many times.

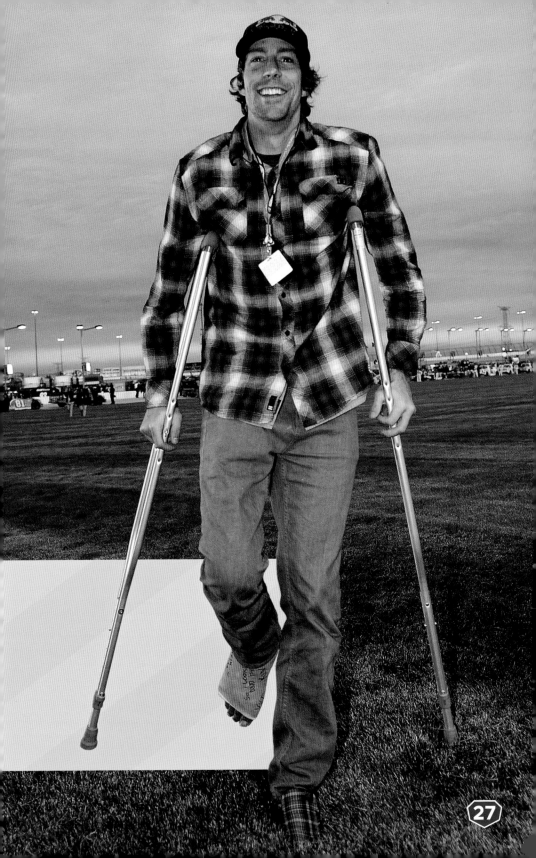

But Travis continues to follow his motto and his heart.

"We practice a lot," says Travis. "And we do our best to make sure everyone stays safe and has fun."

You got this!